Good Health, Better Life

Toshiaki Nishihara
Mayumi Nishihara
Pino Cutrone

KINSEIDO

Kinseido Publishing Co., Ltd.
3-21 Kanda Jimbo-cho, Chiyoda-ku,
Tokyo 101-0051, Japan

Copyright © 2019 by Toshiaki Nishihara
　　　　　　　　　 Mayumi Nishihara
　　　　　　　　　 Pino Cutrone

*All rights reserved. No part of this publication may
be reproduced, stored in a retrieval system, or transmitted,
in any form or by any means, electronic, mechanical,
photocopying, recording or otherwise, without the prior
permission of the publisher.*

First published 2019 by Kinseido Publishing Co., Ltd.

Cover design　Nampoosha Co., Ltd
Text design　　Asahi Media International Inc.
Illustrations　　Toru Igarashi

音声ファイル無料ダウンロード

http://www.kinsei-do.co.jp/download/4078

この教科書で 🎧 DL 00 の表示がある箇所の音声は、上記 URL または QR コードにて無料でダウンロードできます。自習用音声としてご活用ください。

- ▶ PC からのダウンロードをお勧めします。スマートフォンなどでダウンロードされる場合は、ダウンロード前に「解凍アプリ」をインストールしてください。
- ▶ URL は、**検索ボックスではなくアドレスバー (URL 表示欄) に入力**してください。
- ▶ お使いのネットワーク環境によっては、ダウンロードできない場合があります。

◎ CD 00　左記の表示がある箇所の音声は、教室用 CD（Class Audio CD）に収録されています。

はしがき

　本テキストは、「環境と健康」をテーマに私達の日々の健康についてもっと考えてもらいたいという思いから作成されたものです。私達を取り巻く環境や日々の生活習慣が私達の健康に及ぼす影響についての理解を深め、興味関心を喚起できるような題材を精選しました。前作、*Better Health For Every Day* と併せてお使いいただけると、健康に関する知識を深めることができるだけでなく、英語の学びに必要なもの、学びのコツが見えてくるように構成されています。

　各ユニットは、リスニングやリーディング題材の理解に不可欠な語彙学習 Vocabulary Study から始め、Listening Activity、Reading Activity を通して題材となっている事柄への理解を深めていくように構成されています。また、Building Vocabulary through Pictures では、本文中に出てくる基本動詞のイメージの確認と理解を深め、その理解を Vocabulary Exercise と結びつけて題材に関するキーセンテンスを身につけるようにしてあります。テキストの中盤と最後には、復習テスト (Review Test 1, 2) を用意し、学習内容の定着を確認できるようにしました。

　このテキストを通しての学びが、英語力を高めることにつながるとともに健康について考えるきっかけとなれば幸いです。

　なお、拙著の内容については、著者の気づかない不備もあるかと思われます。多くの先生方、利用者からの御教示、御批判をいただければ幸いです。

　最後に、本書の出版に際して、大変お世話になった金星堂の皆さんに心から御礼申し上げます。

著者一同

Good Health, Better Life

Contents

UNIT 1
What Country Is the Fattest in the World? ········ 1
世界で肥満率が高い国

UNIT 2
What Do We Know about Sleep Talking? ········ 7
寝言と睡眠

UNIT 3
Why Are Bug Bites Dangerous? ········ 13
虫刺されに御用心

UNIT 4
What Kind of Bacteria Can Be Found in the Great Barrier Reef? ········ 19
綺麗な海に潜む危険

UNIT 5
How Much Caffeine Can We Take? ········ 25
カフェイン依存の生活の問題

UNIT 6
How Does the Love Hormone Oxytocin Work to Improve Relationships? ········ 31
オキシトシンが関わる人間関係

● Review Test 1 ［Unit 1 ～ Unit 6 復習テスト］········ 37

UNIT 7
What Can Happen When You're Too Clean? ····· 41
潔癖症っていいことづくめ？

UNIT 8
Does Gender Affect Cancer Susceptibility? ····· 47
性差と癌

UNIT 9
Why Do Many of Us Develop Fear of Heights with Age? ······ 53
老化と高所恐怖症

UNIT 10
What Are the Dangers of a Sweltering Summer? ····· 59
夏に潜む危険

UNIT 11
Which Makes a Better Athlete, Being a Night Owl or an Early Bird? ····· 65
スポーツ選手に有利なのは、朝型人間、それとも夜型人間？

UNIT 12
How Better to Release Your Stress? ····· 71
ストレスコントロール

UNIT 13
What Are the Differences between Real and Robotic Pets? ····· 77
ロボペットと本物のペット、どちらを選ぶ？

● Review Test 2 [Unit 7〜Unit 13 復習テスト] ····· 83

UNIT 1

What Country Is the Fattest in the World?

このユニットでは、食事の西洋化がもたらした大きな弊害について考えます。肥満度が高い国がどこかを考えながら学習しましょう。

I VOCABULARY STUDY

次にあげる英語表現の意味を表す日本語を選択肢から選び、記号で答えましょう。

1. obesity [　]
2. soar [　]
3. give up [　]
4. blame [　]
5. diabetes [　]
6. significant [　]
7. prevalence [　]
8. malnutrition [　]
9. outnumber [　]
10. alarming [　]

> a. 糖尿病　　b. 恐怖、警戒感を抱かせる　　c. 肥満　　d. 降参する
> e.（短い時間で）上昇する　　f. 栄養失調　　g. 広がり　　h. 〜に数で勝る
> i. 大きな影響をもつ、意味のある　　j. 〜のせいにする

Ⅱ LISTENING ACTIVITY

会話文を聞きましょう。初めはテキストを見ずに聞き、次にもう一度聞いて空所に英語を書き入れましょう。

In class

Professor: Today we are going to discuss obesity, which is ¹._____ _____ _____ _____ _____ of global significance. What country do you think is the fattest country in the world?

Nina: America has the ²._____ _____ _____ obesity, I think.

Professor: I heard that it wasn't so bad there. Any other ideas?

Nancy: Perhaps you can ³._____ _____ _____ _____?

Professor: Okay, it's a Pacific Island country.

Nina: Well,… I don't have the foggiest idea about it. I give up. Please tell us.

Professor: According to a recently released survey, American Samoa ⁴._____ _____ _____ of obesity. Nauru, a tiny island country, and the Cook Islands located in the South Pacific Ocean, come in second and third places. Their obesity rates are soaring. As a matter of fact, the rates are 71 and 63 percent of the population, respectively.

Nancy: Is that so? How come the obesity rates are so high in those countries?

Professor: Some experts ⁵._____ _____ _____ _____ the westernization of food preferences. The locals in these Pacific Island countries began to eat more fatty and oily food every day.

Nina: Are they ⁶._____ _____ _____ _____ diabetes?

Professor: Indeed. Actually, many people are suffering from it, already.

Nancy: That's a pity! I hope things get better for them in the future.

(203 words)

▶ Listening Comprehension

会話文の内容について、質問に答えましょう。

1. What is the fattest country in the world?
   a. America
   b. Nauru
   c. American Samoa

2. Which is the closest in meaning to "I don't have the foggiest idea."?
   a. I don't have a clue.
   b. I cannot make a decision.
   c. I perfectly understood.

3. What led to the obesity problem in the tropical islands in the Pacific?
   a. Traditional meals contain too much sugar.
   b. The islanders' diet has changed and they've recently been eating western food.
   c. The islanders don't exercise at all.

LISTENING TIPS　　英語のリズムを感じよう　　 DL 04　 CD 04

英語はうねりのある言語だと言われることがあります。大切な単語は強勢がつき文中で「山」となり、長く、強く、高く発音されます。それ以外は短く弱く発音され「谷」となり、その「山－谷」の繰り返しでリズムのうねりができます。次の例では「山」の部分を大文字で示します。

例　I **HEARD** that it **WASN'T** so **BAD** there.

音声を参考に、次の文を英語のリズムを意識して読んでみましょう。

1. I **DON'T** have the **FOGG**iest i**DEA** about it.
2. Their o**BE**sity **RATES** are **SOAR**ing.
3. Some Experts have **BLAMED** it on the **WES**terni**ZA**tion of **FOOD** **PRE**ferences.

Meeting the Challenge of Obesity

Obesity is a significant public health concern around the world. Prevalence rates of obesity-related health problems are increasing in all parts of the world. The problems occur worldwide. Men and women with obesity outnumber those with malnutrition, which was a major health problem in the past.

Regarding the global obesity rankings, the World Health Organization (WHO) recently released some shocking data. Among the top seven are Pacific Island nations. In Nauru, a tiny independent country in the Pacific, for example, 97 percent of men and 93 percent of women are overweight or obese. Three-quarters of the islanders are considered to be clinically obese and 45 percent of those aged 55-64 suffer from diabetes.

These numbers are alarming and this fact indicates that health authorities have to take action to slow the prevalence of obesity in Nauru. The problem is that it is hard for people in Nauru to stay away from a western style diet, which includes tinned beef and mutton. They love eating snacks, which include large portions of fried chicken and excessive amounts of soda. In essence, they are eating themselves to death.

Meanwhile, as far as the obesity rate is concerned, the United States is in seventh place in the obesity rankings. More than 78 percent of Americans are overweight or obese. In Britain, the figure is around 61 percent. In the United States it is expected that one in three can develop diabetes in the near future.

(241 words)

▶ **Reading Comprehension**

本文の内容に合っているものにはTを、合っていないものにはFを選びましょう。

1. Obesity prevalence is not a serious risk to us. [T / F]
2. Forty-five percent of the population of Nauru developed diabetes. [T / F]
3. In the near future in the United States, one-third of the population are at risk of developing diabetes. [T / F]

Ⅳ BUILDING VOCABULARY THROUGH PICTURES

以下の2つの単語が持つイメージをつかみましょう。

soar ＝（短い時間で）高いレベルに上がるイメージ

The planes **soared** through the sky.

The number of applicants **soared**.

stay ＝ある状態の持続 ※keepは、働きかけがあってある状態が持続することを表す。

The weather will **stay** rainy over the next few hours.

I have to **stay** late at work every Tuesday.

V VOCABULARY EXERCISE

前項で学んだ基本動詞を補い、次の日本語に合わせて英語を並び替えましょう。

1. 遠くに雪を被った山々がそびえている。
[mountains, the, in, snow-capped, distance]

2. 期待がいっきに高まり、トンネルの先に光がさすのを覚えた。
[my hopes, I, at the end, the tunnel, and, saw, a light, of]

3. 競争力を持続できるように努力しないといけない。
[I, to, try, have, to, competitive]

Tips on Grammar

1. I don't have the foggiest idea about it.

I haven't <u>got</u> the foggiest/<u>faintest</u> idea about it. とも表現されます。「見当もつかない」という意味の英文ですが、日本人になじみがうすい最上級を用いた英語表現です。他には、次のような最上級を含む英語表現があります。

We have to consider how best to help our students.

The fountain is best visited at night.

Which is your least favorite food?

2. Among the top seven are Pacific Island nations.

この文は、場所を表す語句を文頭の位置においた倒置文ですが、Pacific Island nationsの部分が書き手が「大切な情報」とみなしている部分となります。前置されたamong the top sevenは、前の文の内容・話題をうけ、情報の流れを作っています。

UNIT 2
What Do We Know about Sleep Talking?

寝言と睡眠の関係に触れながら、良い睡眠について理解を深めましょう。

I VOCABULARY STUDY   DL 06   CD 09

次にあげる英語表現の意味を表す日本語を選択肢から選び、記号で答えましょう。

1. prank   [　]　6. disruptive   [　]
2. desperate   [　]　7. doze   [　]
3. Lost and Found   [　]　8. gibberish   [　]
4. progressive   [　]　9. entire   [　]
5. acquire   [　]　10. underlying [　]

> a. 獲得する、得る　b. 絶望的な　c. 破壊的な、混乱を招く
> d. 遺失物取り扱い所　e. 進歩的な　f. 根本的な、基礎をなす
> g. 悪ふざけ　h. うたた寝する　i. 全体の　j. ちんぷんかんぷん（な）

II LISTENING ACTIVITY   DL 07   CD 10

会話文を聞きましょう。初めはテキストを見ずに聞き、次にもう一度聞いて空所に英語を書き入れましょう。

Ken shares the house with Mary and he is lying on the couch.

Ken: "Yawn"

Mary: You ¹·_____ _____ _____ _____.

Ken: Did I?

Mary: A funny thing happened while you were sleeping.

Ken: What? Did you play a prank on me while sleeping?

Mary: No! You were talking in your sleep.

Ken: I had a nightmare that ²·_____ _____ _____ _____ _____ _____ _____. I arrived at SFO on the first flight. When I was going through passport control, I realized that I left my passport somewhere. Then I was ³·_____ _____ looking for my passport.

Mary: What happened next?

Ken: I went to the nearest Lost and Found, but the person at the counter did not understand me. I was ⁴·_____ _____ _____ _____ in English.

Mary: Well, that's a good sign.

Ken: What do you mean?

Mary: Your dream shows that your English is improving.

Ken: How so?

Mary: You were ⁵·_____ _____ _____ _____ that everyone has to go through before acquiring a foreign language. I had a similar dream in French.

Ken: Did you speak French in your sleep?

Mary: Yes, I did. That's what my mother said to me. Don't worry. Sleep talking is a common occurrence, and it's not a medical problem. You are making progress. Try to focus ⁶·_____ _____ _____ _____ _____.

(191 words)

SFO (=San Francisco International Airport)「サンフランシスコ国際空港」

▶ Listening Comprehension

会話文の内容について、質問に答えましょう。

1. How did Ken spend the afternoon?
   a. He slept all afternoon and wasted time.
   b. He took a nap without doing his homework.
   c. He dozed off with the TV on.

2. What experience did Ken have?
   a. He spoke French in his sleep.
   b. He spoke English in his sleep, but he didn't communicate well.
   c. He spoke English fluently in his sleep.

3. What did Mary say about sleep talking?
   a. It is a bad sign.
   b. It is a common thing that many people experience.
   c. It is always a good sign.

LISTENING TIPS リズムの山は「内容語」、谷は「機能語」　DL 08　CD 11

文の中で山となる大切な単語というのは、名詞、動詞、形容詞、副詞、否定語、疑問詞など「内容語」に分類されるものです。反対に a, the などの冠詞、代名詞、前置詞、助動詞などは「機能語」に分類され、ふつうは弱く発音されます。

例 You were **TALK**ing in your **SLEEP**.　←　□ は内容語

次の文の内容語を意識して、読んでみましょう。

1. Then I was **RUSH**ing around **LOOK**ing for my **PASS**port.
2. I **WENT** to the **NEAR**est **LOST** and **FOUND**, but the **PERSON** at the **COUN**ter did **NOT** under**STAND** me.
3. **WHAT** do you **MEAN**?

III READING ACTIVITY

Understanding Sleep Talking

Everyone experiences sleep talking, but strangely enough, little is known about it. Sleep talking is more common in men and children. It rarely requires treatment. Some sleep talking makes no sense and others can be related to your past events and experiences. Although it is not physically harmful in many cases, it can annoy a bed partner or roommate, and it can be very disruptive in group-sleeping situations.

Sleep talking can occur in both REM and non-REM sleep. Regarding non-REM sleep, there are three stages. In light sleep (in REM sleep and Stage 1 of non-REM sleep), people 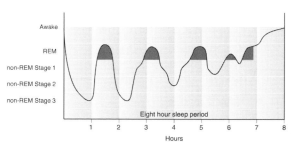 can have entire conversations with the people in their dreams. Their sleep talking can be comprehensible to the people near them. In contrast, in the deep sleep stage (in Stage 2 and 3 of non-REM sleep), speech may sound gibberish.

Severe sleep talking may be the result of another more serious sleep disorder or medical condition. Keep a sleep diary so that you can identify your sleep patterns and habits. After you are aware of your sleep patterns, see your doctor for help to find out if an underlying problem is causing your sleep talking. Keep a sleep diary for two weeks. Note the times you go to bed, when you think you fell asleep, and when you woke up. In addition, it is useful to monitor the following things as well.

☐ Caffeine consumption   ☐ Alcohol consumption   ☐ Food consumption
☐ Stress   ☐ Exercise   ☐ Medications

Learning about your sleep patterns may be the key to treating a sleep disorder if you have one.

(256 words)

REM「急速眼球運動」(rapid eye movement)
脳の覚醒状態が維持されており、眼球が左右に動く状況の眠りを指し、それぞれの単語の頭文字をとってREM (レム) 睡眠と呼ばれる。レム＝浅い睡眠、ノンレム＝深い睡眠

▶ **Reading Comprehension**

本文の内容に合っているものにはTを、合っていないものにはFを選びましょう。

1. Sleep talking is more common in women. [T / F]
2. Sleep talking can occur during any stage of non-REM sleep. [T / F]
3. When you think that sleep talking may come from a sleeping disorder, keeping a sleep diary is useful. [T / F]

Ⅳ BUILDING VOCABULARY THROUGH PICTURES

以下の2つの単語が持つイメージをつかみましょう。

 arrive　＝人・物が届くイメージ／ある場所や地位などにたどり着くイメージ

We arrived at the same conclusion.

The package has just arrived.

 **run**　＝一定のスピードで進む ➡ 機能する

The bus runs between Tokyo and Nagoya.

Artistic talent runs in my family.

V VOCABULARY EXERCISE

前項で学んだ基本動詞を補い、次の日本語に合わせて英語を並び替えましょう。

1. 私たちの家具は、無事に昨日届いた。
   [our, yesterday, furniture, safely]

   _____

2. 彼女がその大学に准教授としての職を得たのは、まだ32歳の時だった。
   [when, an, at, associate, the university, as, professor, she]
   She was just 32 _____.

3. 寝言を言うのは、私の家系に見られる。
   [my, sleep, in, talking, family]

   _____

Tips on Grammar

1. I slept the afternoon away.

time-away構文と呼ばれるタイプの文です。主語と動詞の部分が行為を表し、その行為の結果特定の時間が過ぎ去ったことを表します。We talked the night away.（私たちは語り明かした）

2. I arrived at Nagasaki Station.

arriveの後にatを用いる場合、駅や空港など経由地を指します。すでに街中にいるような場合、This is just to tell you that I have arrived in Nagasaki. のようにinを用います。

3. Our furniture is constructed with high-quality fabrics.

furnitureは、不可算名詞扱いをします。

UNIT 3

Why Are Bug Bites Dangerous?

単なる虫刺されだと侮るのは危険です。私たちに身近な場所に存在する虫とウィルスについて理解を深めましょう。

I VOCABULARY STUDY   DL 10   CD 15

次にあげる英語表現の意味を表す日本語を選択肢から選び、記号で答えましょう。

1. well-tended [　]
2. vitality [　]
3. sprout [　]
4. sting [　]
5. excruciating [　]
6. contagious [　]
7. viral [　]
8. defect [　]
9. accompany [　]
10. repellent [　]

a. 生命力	b. よく手入れされた	c. 障害	d. 芽を出す	e. 刺すこと、刺す
f. 感染する	g. ウィルス性の	h. ひどく痛い	i. 防虫剤	j. 伴う

II LISTENING ACTIVITY   DL 11   CD 16

会話文を聞きましょう。初めはテキストを見ずに聞き、次にもう一度聞いて空所に英語を書き入れましょう。

Angie: What a beautiful and well-tended garden!

Peter: Thank you. My hobby is gardening and I enjoy observing 1._____ _____ _____ _____ _____. When plants sprout from seeds and 2._____ _____ _____ _____, I feel the vitality of life. I am happy when I find something blooming.

Angie: I feel the same way. Gardening is a lot of fun. It's a creative, ongoing process. Digging, planting, weeding, and pruning 3._____ _____ _____. Do you know that 30 minutes of active gardening burns up to 280 kilocalories?

Peter: Really, that much?

Angie: By gardening you can stay fit. In order to enjoy healthy gardening, here is a tip for you. 4._____ _____ _____ _____ _____ from bugs in the wild.

Peter: Why? Have you had any painful experiences?

Angie: Yes. There are caterpillars 5._____ _____ _____. They pack a big sting and it hurts. I was bitten by one last year and it was excruciating.

Peter: Talking about bug bites, Dengue fever and Zika fever are spreading around the world. In Brazil, expecting mothers infected with Zika virus can sometimes 6._____ _____ with microcephaly. It is a big health issue now.

Angie: Is it? We better avoid mosquito bites.

(188 words)

microcephaly「小頭症」

▶ Listening Comprehension

会話文の内容について、質問に答えましょう。

1. What is Peter's hobby?
    a. do-it-yourself
    b. gardening
    c. flower arrangement

2. How many calories can 30 minutes of gardening burn up?
    a. no more than 280 kilocalories
    b. 300 kilocalories
    c. 400 kilocalories

3. Which birth defect can Zika virus cause?
    a. abnormal smallness of head circumference
    b. a small bowel obstruction
    c. small damaged vessels

LISTENING TIPS　機能語 and の音変化　

強弱のリズムの「谷」にくる「機能語」は、元々の単語の発音どおりには発音されないことが多く、聞き取りが難しくなります。ここでは and に焦点をあててどのように発音が変わるのか見てみましょう。

例　I enjoy observing living things and life cycles.
→ and の最初の a の音は前の単語の語末音 s とつながり、最後の d の音は、発音されず落とされます。

次の文の and の発音に着目し、読んでみましょう。

1. beautiful and well-tended garden
2. plants sprout from seeds and climb
3. last year and it was excruciating
4. Dengue fever and Zika fever

III READING ACTIVITY

Unfamiliar Infectious Diseases

In recent years, the news about two unfamiliar diseases caught our attention. One is Zika fever, and the other is Dengue fever. These are contagious diseases carried by mosquitoes. Both Zika virus and Dengue virus are transmitted by female mosquitoes mainly of the species Aedes aegypti.

When the 2016 Olympic Games were held in Rio de Janeiro, Brazil, Zika fever emerged as a major public health problem in Brazil, and medical experts in many countries issued guidance for people who were planning to travel to the area, saying that Aedes species mosquitoes are active during both the daytime and nighttime. Zika virus can be passed from a pregnant woman to her fetus and infection during pregnancy can cause birth defects such as microcephaly.

Dengue is a mosquito-borne viral infection. The disease is common in some parts of Asia such as Taiwan and Southeast Asia, but it is no longer limited to tropical and subtropical areas as global travel becomes commonplace. The global incidence of Dengue fever has grown dramatically in recent decades. About half of the world population is now at risk. Sufferers of Dengue fever experience a sudden fever that continues three to seven days, accompanied by head and muscle pain and a rash.

The recent outbreak of Zika fever in Brazil and Dengue fever in Tokyo are still fresh in our minds. Since there is no specific treatment and no vaccine commercially available against these diseases, do what you can do: wear protective clothing and use mosquito repellent to prevent infection. (253 words)

Aedes aegypti
「ネッタイシマカ(ヤブ蚊の一種)」

▶ Reading Comprehension

本文の内容に合っているものにはTを、合っていないものにはFを選びましょう。

1. Two familiar infectious diseases drew our attention. [T / F]
2. Zika virus infection during pregnancy can cause birth defects. [T / F]
3. Due to advanced medical technologies, there are some treatments available against Zika and Dengue viruses. [T / F]

Ⅳ BUILDING VOCABULARY THROUGH PICTURES

以下の2つの単語が持つイメージをつかみましょう。

 ＝徐々に上がるイメージ

The plane climbed higher and higher.

The temperature climbed to 40 degrees.

 ＝ある対象の移動に伴って、別の対象も移動するイメージ

This bus carries 40 people.

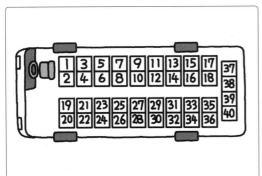

Mosquitoes can carry diseases.

Unit 3 Why Are Bug Bites Dangerous?

V VOCABULARY EXERCISE

前項で学んだ基本動詞を補い、次の日本語に合わせて英語を並び替えましょう。

1. 失業率が徐々に上がった。
   [steadily, unemployment]
   _____

2. その道は、徐々に山に向かって上り坂になっている。
   [the, up, the mountain, road]
   _____

3. 彼女は、肩にバッグをかけていた。
   [was, her, bag, her, over, shoulder]
   She _____.

Tips on Grammar

1. I am happy when I find something blooming.

findのあとに名詞句が続き、さらに形容詞の類が続く場合は直接的な経験を表します。例えば、I found the chair comfortable.では、実際にいすに座って快適さを経験していることになります。他方、I found that the chair was comfortable.では、広告などの情報などから判断して快適であることがわかった場合に用います。

2. Remember to protect your skin.

動詞rememberには、-ingとto doの形を続けることができますが、意味の違いに注意が必要です。-ingでは「〜したことを覚えている」という意味に対して、remember to doでは「忘れずに〜してください」という意味になります。

3. There are caterpillars crawling around vegetation.

There—動詞—名詞句の連鎖のあとには、-ing、過去分詞、(一時的な状態を表す) 形容詞を入れることも可能です。There are a lot of people involved in that decision. / There are some people sick.などのように表現できます。

UNIT 4

What Kind of Bacteria Can Be Found in the Great Barrier Reef?

美しいサンゴ礁の海にも危険が存在することを学び、自分で自分を守る術を学びましょう。

I VOCABULARY STUDY   DL 14   CD 22

次にあげる英語表現の意味を表す日本語を選択肢から選び、記号で答えましょう。

1. coral cay   [   ]   6. raw   [   ]
2. surrounded by   [   ]   7. amputate   [   ]
3. magnificent   [   ]   8. infected   [   ]
4. exposed   [   ]   9. contract   [   ]
5. contaminate   [   ]   10. attribute   [   ]

> **a.** 生の **b.** 珊瑚でできた小島 **c.** 汚染する **d.** とてもすばらしい **e.** 感染した
> **f.** 危険などにさらされる **g.** 〜に帰する、〜と考える **h.** 比較的重い病気にかかる
> **i.** 〜に囲まれている **j.** 外科手術で体の一部を切断する

II LISTENING ACTIVITY

会話文を聞きましょう。初めはテキストを見ずに聞き、次にもう一度聞いて空所に英語を書き入れましょう。

Alfred: Hi.

Lisa: Hi. Everything fine?

Alfred: I'm doing okay. How about you?

Lisa: Pretty good. Thank you. Summer vacation is 1._____ _____ _____ . What's your plan for the coming vacation?

Alfred: I'm going to the Great Barrier Reef in Northern Australia. I'm planning 2._____ _____ _____ _____ _____ _____ Green Island. There is a beautiful coral cay in the Great Barrier Reef, 3._____ _____ white sandy beaches and magnificent coral reefs. Just about a 45-minute boat ride from Cairns.

Lisa: Sounds exciting.

Alfred: Regarding the area, I just read a paper. It says one type of the flesh-eating bacteria, Vibrio vulnificus, was found in the Great Barrier Reef.

Lisa: Sounds scary.

Alfred: It is in the same family of bacteria that causes Cholera. The bacteria is found in warm, shallow salt water and it can infect our bodies through an open wound exposed to contaminated sea water.

Lisa: Thank you for the updated information about the bacteria and the area.

Alfred: 4._____ _____ _____ _____ _____ when you have an open wound.

Lisa: Sure. Does the bacteria exist in the sea around Japan, too?

Alfred: Sure it does. It was found in Japan. 5._____ _____ _____ , not many doctors have a basic knowledge about the bacteria.

Lisa: Oh, that's a big problem!

(199 words)

▶ Listening Comprehension

会話文の内容について、質問に答えましょう。

1. Where is Green Island located?
   a. in the Caribbean Sea
   b. in the Great Barrier Reef in Southern Australia
   c. in the Great Barrier Reef in Northern Australia

2. What is Vibrio vulnificus?
   a. It is a virus.
   b. It is in the family of flu viruses.
   c. It is a man-eating bacteria.

3. How does the bacteria infect people?
   a. through exposure to contaminated food
   b. through an open wound
   c. through droplet infection

LISTENING TIPS　音変化①　融合同化　

隣り合う音が混じり合って新しい音が生まれる現象を融合同化といいます。ここでは、yで始まる単語が、前の単語の最後の音と融合する音変化を見ていきましょう。

例　Thank you.

次の文の同化を意識して、読んでみましょう。

1. How about you?
2. What's your plan?
3. Avoid swimming in water when you have an open wound.

III READING ACTIVITY

The Risk of Eating Sea Food

Many people like eating raw oysters, and raw oyster bars are growing in popularity both at home and abroad. However, people are usually unaware of dangerous bacteria that exist in oysters. Eating undercooked or uncooked oysters can put you at risk of bacterial infections, including Vibrio bacteria.

Vibrio bacteria thrive in coastal salt water and live in oysters. Since oysters feed by filtering water, the bacteria can concentrate in their tissues. Oysters, which contain these harmful bacteria, do not look, smell, or even taste different from any other oyster. Therefore, a better idea is to avoid eating raw oysters so that you will not be infected with the bacteria.

According to CDC in the U.S., the bacteria cause about 45,000 cases of disease each year in the country, and 86% of which are food-borne gastroenteritis. Vibrio vulnificus not only causes food-borne illness but wound-related illness. Wounds account for 60% of all Vibrio vulnificus cases in the U.S., and every year many people contract Vibrio while fishing. In Florida, there were nine deaths in 2012 and 13 deaths in 2011 attributed to the bacteria. In some cases, people infected with the bacteria had to have their legs amputated.

Regarding the Vibrio vulnificus bacterium in particular, not many doctors have a basic knowledge about the bacteria, and they do not know about effective treatments for the bacterial infection. Here is a tip for you! Have a working knowledge of the environments around you. Otherwise, you might become infected with this dreadful bacteria.

(250 words)

CDC (=Center for Disease Control and Prevention)「アメリカ疾病予防管理センター」
gastroenteritis「胃腸炎」
Vibrio vulnificus「ビブリオ・バルニフィカス」(ビブリオ科に属する菌で、人喰いバクテリアと呼ばれる)

▶ **Reading Comprehension**

本文の内容に合っているものにはTを、合っていないものにはFを選びましょう。

1. Uncooked oysters are completely safe. [T / F]
2. Vibrio vulnificus causes food and wound-related illnesses. [T / F]
3. Physicians have a complete understanding of Vibrio vulnificus. [T / F]

Ⅳ BUILDING VOCABULARY THROUGH PICTURES

以下の2つの単語が持つイメージをつかみましょう。

 ＝開く・開いているイメージ 「幕が開く」 ☞ 開始イメージ

The sky opened up.

The doors opened at 7:00 pm.

concentrate ＝何かが集中していたり、意識、研究、努力などを集中させるイメージ

Concentrate your academic studies in linguistics.

Major development has been concentrated in and around cities.

V   VOCABULARY EXERCISE

前項で学んだ基本動詞を補い、次の日本語に合わせて英語を並び替えましょう。

1. 野球の試合は、国歌斉唱で始まった。
   [National Anthem, the, with, baseball game, the]
   _____

2. そのショーは、スケジュール通りに始まった。
   [the, schedule, on, show]
   _____

3. 英語の勉強に努力を傾注する必要があります。
   [need, your, efforts, to]
   You _____ on learning English.

Tips on Grammar

1. The problem is, not many doctors have a basic knowledge about the bacteria.

The problem is, ... / The truth is, ...などの表現は、「問題はというと」「実のところ」という意味を表す前置き表現です。The problem is, ...の形式だけでなく、thatを伴って、The problem is that he is always late.（問題はというと、彼がいつも遅れることなのです）のように、表現することも可能です。

2. Sure it does. It was found in Japan.

本来は、副詞surelyを用いる場面で、口語体ではIt sure is cold.やIt sure is an honor.のように、sureを用いることがあります。Kei Nishikori is an incredible tennis player, that's for sure.のような文に見られる決まり文句that's for sure.の使い方にも慣れましょう。

UNIT 5

How Much Caffeine Can We Take?

カフェインがもたらす作用について学び、適度な摂取量を取るように心がけましょう。

I VOCABULARY STUDY

次にあげる英語表現の意味を表す日本語を選択肢から選び、記号で答えましょう。

1. caffeinated [ ]
2. energize [ ]
3. nutritional [ ]
4. tremendous [ ]
5. chronic [ ]
6. trigger [ ]
7. stimulant [ ]
8. tolerance [ ]
9. adverse [ ]
10. life-threatening [ ]

> a. 慢性の b. 許容量 c. 引き金になる d. 刺激作用のある、刺激剤
> e. 栄養上の f. ものすごい、恐ろしい g. 生命に関わる h. 有害な
> i. 精力的にする j. カフェインが含まれる

II   LISTENING ACTIVITY   DL 19   CD 30

会話文を聞きましょう。初めはテキストを見ずに聞き、次にもう一度聞いて空所に英語を書き入れましょう。

At a host family house

Keita: Morning.

Mrs. Thomson: Morning. Would you like to have some coffee?

Keita: Yes, please. In Japan I always **1.**_____ _____ _____ _____ with a cup of coffee. (*Smelling and tasting*) This coffee is fragrant.

Mrs. Thomson: It's Kona Coffee from the Big Island in Hawaii.

Keita: I see.

Mrs. Thomson: After drinking some caffeinated coffee, I **2.**_____ _____ and I can concentrate on my work.

Keita: I agree. **3.**_____ _____ _____ _____ _____ _____ _____, many people drink it, and it is in fact the second most consumed beverage worldwide next to plain water. However, some experts feel that too much caffeine is not a good idea.

Mrs. Thomson: Why is that?

Keita: Caffeine overdose is a big issue these days. It has tremendous **4.**_____ _____ _____ _____ bodies. According to a recently released news story, a young Japanese boy died from overdosing on energy drinks. Apparently, he drank caffeinated drinks so that he could stay awake. He was a student who worked hard to support himself and became unconscious and **5.**_____ _____ while he was working part time.

Mrs. Thomson: Poor boy. Probably, the effects of chronic caffeine intake damaged his health.

Keita: Another case was reported in the U.S. A girl, who drank mixed energy drinks, passed away. We'd **6.**_____ _____ _____ _____ our caffeine intake.

(203 words)

▶ Listening Comprehension

会話文の内容について、質問に答えましょう。

1. What did Keita start his day with?
   a. a cup of tea
   b. a cup of aromatic coffee
   c. a cup of weak coffee

2. What is the most consumed beverage in the world?
   a. plain water
   b. coffee
   c. soft drinks

3. What happened to the Japanese boy?
   a. He vomited many times.
   b. He fainted away entirely.
   c. After he lost consciousness, he passed away.

LISTENING TIPS	音変化②　連結（リンキング）　 DL 20　 CD 31

単語の最後の音が子音で、次の単語が母音で始まる時に、2つの音が繋がって発音される現象を連結といいます。自然な英語では多く見られます。

例　I usually start my day off with a cup of coffee.

次の文の連結を意識して、読んでみましょう。

1. Many people like coffee. I also love it and drink it every day.
2. It has negative effects on us.
3. We should be careful about our health.
4. The effects of chronic caffeine intake are the cause of the illness.

III READING ACTIVITY

Caffeine Intake and Sleepless Problems

In this modern world, many people are stuck in a vicious cycle. They are suffering from sleeplessness, and as a result, their work performance suffers. Poor sleep also harms their concentration. In order to concentrate on their work, they consume caffeinated drinks.

Many people, however, are not aware of the risk of caffeine overdose. They do not see the dangers that medical experts see. Caffeine is a stimulant drug, and it is a chemical that affects our central nervous system. It elevates our heart rate. Taking in too much caffeine can trigger breathing trouble, confusion, convulsions, and an irregular heartbeat.

More importantly, energy drinks that include caffeine have numerous ingredients and each of these produces a different action in the body. These ingredients include stimulants, antidepressants, and anti-anxiety agents, so taking too much caffeine mixed with other ingredients may cause a more serious health risk. Moderate intake of energy drinks is safe, but those with a high dose of caffeine must be avoided.

Energy drinks are everywhere these days, and they are marketed and sold alongside soft drinks at convenience stores. They are easily obtained, so we have to be cautious about not drinking too much caffeine. Although allergic reactions to caffeine depend on individual tolerance, we have to understand caffeine sensitivity. According to doctors in the Mayo Clinic, the recommended amount of caffeine is normally 200-400mg daily for healthy adults. This amount of caffeine does not usually lead to an adverse reaction. Remember a caffeine overdose can be life-threatening.

(250 words)

antidepressants「抗うつ薬」

▶ **Reading Comprehension**

本文の内容に合っているものにはTを、合っていないものにはFを選びましょう。

1. Many people are suffering from sleep-related problems. [T / F]
2. Beside caffeine, energy drinks include other ingredients such as stimulants and antidepressants. [T / F]
3. You shouldn't drink more than 400 mg of caffeine a day for a healthy life. [T / F]

Ⅳ BUILDING VOCABULARY THROUGH PICTURES

以下の2つの単語が持つイメージをつかみましょう。

 ＝Aを起点に「何らかの動作や行為が始まる・始まる」イメージ

The river starts in the Yukon, Canada and flows through Alaska.

School starts in late September.

 ＝「存在しなくなる」「生命活動がなくなる」イメージ

Our love will never die.

Old habits die hard.

Ⅴ VOCABULARY EXERCISE

前項で学んだ基本動詞を補い、次の日本語に合わせて英語を並び替えましょう。

1. 無料のガイド付きツアーから私の訪問をスタートさせた。
   [my, a, tour, visit, with, free guided]
   I _____.

2. 彼らの母語が消滅しつつある。
   [their, language, is, out, native]
   _____

3. 酸性雨の影響で多くの木が完全に枯れつつある。
   [many, are, trees, acid rain, from]
   _____

Tips on Grammar

1. He died from overwork.

「〜で亡くなる」という日本語には、die from / die ofを用います。直接的な原因の場合はdie ofを用い、間接的な要因と考えられるものにdie fromを用いる傾向が見られますが、両者を区別しない英語母語話者も多くいます。例えば、死亡要因が、hunger、cancer、a heart attackなどは、of / fromどちらでも可能です。人が「亡くなる」ことを婉曲的に表現するのがpass awayです。イギリス英語では、go for a Burtonという表現もあります。

2. Chronic fatigue syndrome is a complicated illness characterized by at least six months of extreme fatigue.

chronicのあとには、pain、disease(s)、fatigueなど健康に関わる名詞が続きますが、chronic problem、chronic shortage、chronic povertyのように表現することも可能です。

UNIT 6
How Does the Love Hormone Oxytocin Work to Improve Relationships?

ラブホルモンと呼ばれるオキシトシンについての理解を深めましょう。また、女性のコミュニケーションの特徴についても学びましょう。

I   VOCABULARY STUDY   DL 22   CD 36

次にあげる英語表現の意味を表す日本語を選択肢から選び、記号で答えましょう。

1. facilitate   [   ]   6. neurotransmitter   [   ]
2. attachment   [   ]   7. secrete   [   ]
3. identify   [   ]   8. pituitary gland   [   ]
4. kinship   [   ]   9. explore   [   ]
5. description   [   ]   10. potential   [   ]

> a. 探る   b. 愛着、愛情   c. 分泌する   d. 神経伝達物質   e. 脳下垂体
> f. 促進する   g. 記述、描写   h. 血族、同族関係   i. 潜在的な
> j. 〜に相違ないと確認する

II LISTENING ACTIVITY DL 23 CD 37

会話文を聞きましょう。初めはテキストを見ずに聞き、次にもう一度聞いて空所に英語を書き入れましょう。

Toshi: What are you reading?

Amy: This? It's a book written by Deborah Tannen, a professor at Georgetown University in the U.S.

Toshi: 1. _____ _____ _____ _____ ?

Amy: To put it briefly, the professor points out that there is a huge gap in conversation styles between men and women. This book gives a good description of the 2. _____ _____ _____ of men and women.

Toshi: How are they different?

Amy: The book includes an episode in which a wife was quite surprised by her husband's attitude change. The husband, who didn't speak much at home, turned into a talkative man in public. The book shows men do the public speaking.

Toshi: Sounds interesting. 3. _____ _____ _____ _____ book. Understanding gender differences is the key to establishing and strengthening relationships.

Amy: Right.

Toshi: I am now reading a book on love hormones. As far as I understand, some hormones facilitate women to identify kinship and 4. _____ _____ towards others. They drive most of what women feel.

Amy: How can we release love hormones?

Toshi: Just imagine hugging someone you love.

Amy: What else?

Toshi: Think of creative ways to 5. _____ _____ _____. A friend of mine followed these simple practices, and they 6. _____ _____ _____ her life. They really work.

Amy: You're kidding.

(199 words)

▶ Listening Comprehension

会話文の内容について、質問に答えましょう。

1. What does the book by Professor Tannen describe?
    a. different communication styles preferred by men and women
    b. communication breakdown between people from different countries
    c. meanings of non-verbal cues

2. In what situation do many men become talkative?
    a. at home
    b. in public
    c. at any place

3. When are love hormones released?
    a. thinking about future opportunities
    b. thinking of positive ways to help people who are in trouble
    c. thinking of what you have keen interest in

LISTENING TIPS　音変化③　脱落　　DL 24　CD 38

単語の最後の破裂音 (p,t,k,b,d,g) は、次の単語が母音で始まらない場合は連結できず、音が脱落し聞こえなくなります。

例 This book gives a good description of the preferred communication styles.

次の文の脱落を意識して、読んでみましょう。

1. A wife was quite surprised by her husband's attitude change.
2. Sounds like a must-read book.
3. The hormones facilitate women to promote tolerance towards others.
4. Think of creative ways to help people in need.

III READING ACTIVITY

Love and the Brain

Helen Fisher at Rutgers University in the United States claims that love has three stages: Lust, Attraction, and Attachment. In the first stage, the two sex hormones testosterone and estrogen drive both men and women to love. The hormones involved in the second stage are adrenaline, dopamine and serotonin.
5 In the feeling of attachment, two major hormones are involved. They are oxytocin and vasopressin, both of which work together with dopamine to form the pair bonds.

Oxytocin is widely referred to as the love hormone. It acts as a hormone and neurotransmitter. It is secreted by the part of our brain named the pituitary
10 gland. A high level of oxytocin is observed in couples in the first six months of a romantic relationship. The hormone is also active after mothers give birth. Oxytocin facilitates childbirth and breast-feeding.

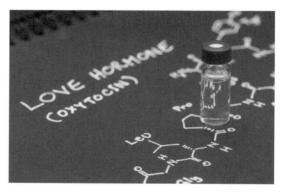

The behavioral effects of oxytocin are reported in recent research on the
15 hormone. A 2013 research paper in the Proceedings of the National Academy of Sciences (PNAS) explored the behavioral effects of oxytocin. It compared the brain scans of men who
20 received the hormone with those that received a placebo. The results demonstrated that oxytocin was associated not only with activation of men's brains, but with greater feelings of attraction to their partners.

Now you understand the reasons why oxytocin is called the 'love hormone.'
25 Scientists are still busy testing potential effects of the hormone.

(232 words)

Proceedings of the National Academy of Sciences (PNAS)「米国科学アカデミー紀要」(米国科学アカデミーが発行する機関誌)

▶ **Reading Comprehension**

本文の内容に合っているものにはTを、合っていないものにはFを選びましょう。

1. According to the text, love has four stages. [T / F]
2. The hormone that we call love hormone is dopamine. [T / F]
3. Oxytocin has effects on our feelings. [T / F]

IV BUILDING VOCABULARY THROUGH PICTURES

以下の2つの単語が持つイメージをつかみましょう。

 ＝何かが生じる元を生み出すイメージ

They established a good relationship.

The system is well-established.

 ＝何かを前に推し進めるイメージ

He has a lot of drive.

A fear drove him to leave.

V VOCABULARY EXERCISE

前項で学んだ基本動詞を補い、次の日本語に合わせて英語を並び替えましょう。

1. スタンフォード大学は、1885年に創立された。
   [was, in 1885, Stanford University]
   _____

2. 最近の問題が生じる随分と前から彼女の評判は、もっぱら不注意者だとされていた。
   [her, for, was, carelessness, reputation]
   _____ long before the latest problem arose.

3. 彼は、好奇心からアボリジニーの文化について学ぶことにした。
   [Aboriginal culture, learn, him, curiosity, to, about]
   _____

Tips on Grammar

1. This book gives a good description of the preferred communication styles of men and women.

「この本を読めば〜」「この本には〜が書かれている」という日本語を英語に直す場合、this bookを主語にして作文できるようにしましょう。descriptionの代わりに、idea, account, overview, summaryなどを用いることもできます。

2. Oxytocin is widely referred to as the love hormone.

refer to A as B / regard A as B / see [view] A as B / describe A as Bなども使えるようになりましょう。

Review Test 1

Unit 1～6で学習してきた内容の復習テストです。各ユニットの内容を思い出しながら、それぞれの問題に答えましょう。

Part 1

LisaとKenの会話を聞きましょう。
会話の内容に合っているものにはTを、合っていないものにはFを選びましょう。
7～10は質問の答えとして正しい選択肢を選びましょう。

CD 43

1. Ken is happy because he began to learn to cook. [T / F]
2. Ken is worrying about his weight. [T / F]
3. Ken is suffering from diabetes. [T / F]
4. There are many attractive advertisements about food around us. [T / F]
5. Lisa thinks Ken has a small appetite. [T / F]
6. Ken decided to change his eating habits to keep his body in good condition. [T / F]
7. What's Lisa's advice?
    a. Ken should be aware of what he is eating so that he can save money.
    b. Ken should learn about nutritional facts so that he can get a cooking license.
    c. Ken should be conscious about the food that he eats so that he can stay healthy.
8. What is Ken's attitude toward *Washoku*?
    a. He hates it.
    b. He is very interested in it and likes it very much.
    c. He is uninterested in cooking.
9. Why does Ken want to have a *Washoku* party?
    a. He wants to show how good his cooking skills are.
    b. He wants to offer *Washoku* to elderly people.
    c. He wants to provide an opportunity for his friends to enjoy *Washoku* with all their senses.
10. What's Ken's suggestion when Lisa comes to the party?
    a. She should bring the best sauce for *Washoku*.
    b. She doesn't have to bring anything for the party.
    c. She should bring some of her friends to the party.

Review Test 1

Part 2

英文を読み、質問に答えましょう。　　　CD 44 ～ CD 46

Superbug

Scientists have found a superbug in the drinking water of New Deli, India. The bug is called NDM-1 and it is notoriously hard to treat with drugs. It is resistant to antibiotics. More surprisingly, NDM-1 was found in seepage water, that is, the water that children may play in on streets.

NDM-1 is spreading around the world through a variety of means and can be transferred due to poor food preparation, global tourism, and medical procedures. In Japan, the nation's first case of NDM-1 infection was reported in 2009. A 54-year-old Japanese man, who traveled to India for business, was infected with the superbug. The gene in the bacteria can produce the disease bacteria and make enzymes to fight against effective antibiotics. Antibiotics are the main medical treatment for bacterial infections.

The emergence of antibiotic-resistant bacteria is a threat to public health, so there is a growing concern about the possibility that NDM-1 can spread worldwide. If this situation occurs, it will be a pandemic. A pandemic is an occurrence of a disease that affects many people over a wide area throughout an entire country, continent, or the whole world.

(190 words)

英文の内容に合っているものにはTを、合っていないものにはFを選びましょう。

1. NDM-1 is easy to treat with antibiotics. [T / F]
2. No cases of NDM-1 infections have been reported in Japan. [T / F]
3. NDM-1 is characterized as a disease bacteria that make enzymes that are resistant to antibiotics. [T / F]
4. There is a mounting concern that NDM-1 can be easily transferred. [T / F]
5. A pandemic is an occurrence of a locally produced disease. [T / F]

Part 3

英文の（　　）に入る適切な語を選択肢から選びましょう。

1. Obesity is a (　　) public health concern around the world.

2. People in Nauru can hardly (　　) away from a western style diet.

3. Sleep talking (　　) requires treatment.

4. In recent years, Zika fever (　　) as a major public health problem in Brazil.

5. Eating (　　) or uncooked oysters can put you at risk of bacteria infections.

6. In Florida, there were nine deaths in 2012 (　　) to the bacteria.

7. Many people are not (　　) of risks of caffeine overdose.

8. Caffeine (　　) our heart rate.

9. A 2013 research paper in the Proceedings of the National Academy Science (PNAS) (　　) the behavioral effects of oxytocin.

10. Oxytocin is widely (　　) to as the love hormone.

a. attributed	b. aware	c. elevates	d. emerged	e. explored
f. rarely	g. occur	h. referred	i. significant	j. stay
k. undercooked				

Review Test 1

Part 4

日本語に合わせて、(　)に適切な語を書き入れましょう。

1. その歌手の人気は、一気に高まった。
   The singer's popularity (s   ).

2. 暴風を伴う天候のために、飛行機は地上に待機したままだった。
   Planes (s   ) on the ground for a few hours because of the stormy weather.

3. 私たちは、新しく来た外国人留学生のためにパーティを開いた。
   We had a party for a newly (a   ) overseas student.

4. 彼が帰宅してみると、流しに水が流れっぱなしだった。
   The water was (r   ) in the sink when he got home.

5. その道路は、山麓丘陵に向かって上り坂です。
   The road (c   ) into the foothills of the mountains.

6. その展示会は、昨日一般公開された。
   The exhibition (o   ) to the public yesterday.

7. 学習目標に到達できるように、集中して努力しなさい。
   (C   ) your efforts on reaching your learning goals.

8. 偏見というものは、なかなか無くならない。
   Prejudice (d   ) hard.

9. さっさとできる運動から1日を始めましょう。
   (S   ) the day with a quick workout.

10. 誰が市場を活性化させて成長へと導いたのですか。
    Who (d   ) the economy into growth?

UNIT 7

What Can Happen When You're Too Clean?

綺麗にしすぎることがかえって良くないこともあることを学習しましょう。

I VOCABULARY STUDY   DL 26   CD 47

次にあげる英語表現の意味を表す日本語を選択肢から選び、記号で答えましょう。

1. air purifier [ ]
2. sort out [ ]
3. hygiene [ ]
4. verify [ ]
5. freak [ ]
6. credible [ ]
7. immune-related [ ]
8. microbe [ ]
9. deprive [ ]
10. susceptible [ ]

> a. 説明する、確かめる   b. 空気清浄機   c. 微生物   d. 心酔者、変人
> e. 免疫と関連がある   f. 感染しやすい、影響を受けやすい   g. 信用できる
> h. 整理する   i. 衛生   j. 奪う

II LISTENING ACTIVITY

会話文を聞きましょう。初めはテキストを見ずに聞き、次にもう一度聞いて空所に英語を書き入れましょう。

Amy: What a messy room! And so dusty, too. How many times do I have to tell you to keep your room clean?

Ken: I cleaned my room last week, and I know where things are. They are 1._____ _____ _____ _____ , I guess. Besides, I sometimes turn the air purifier on.

Amy: Where is your vacuum cleaner? Go get it. Open the window, will you? While I am sweeping your room, 2._____ _____ _____ . You're bad at organizing things. You need to be a more organized person.

Ken: Okay. But you know what? Too clean is actually not always a good thing.

Amy: What do you mean? What are you talking about? Home hygiene is important.

Ken: Well, some scientists believe 3._____ _____ _____ _____ bacteria may be 4._____ _____ _____ in allergic reactions.

Amy: Is that true?

Ken: Yeah. You're too obsessed with cleanliness. You're a neat freak. You're obsessed with hand washing, too. Too much washing damages the normal flora, 5._____ _____ _____ _____ by competing with harmful organisms.

Amy: What! You are full of good excuses.

Ken: All we need is timely cleaning and not excessive cleaning. Too much cleaning 6._____ _____ _____ _____ too little cleaning.   (192 words)

normal flora「正常フローラ、正常細菌叢」
（人体に常在する細菌をいう）

▶ Listening Comprehension

会話文の内容について、質問に答えましょう。

1. What type of person does Ken regard Amy to be?
   a. a strict mother
   b. a poor organizer
   c. a neat freak

2. What is one of the possible reasons for the rise in allergic reactions?
   a. excessive physical contact with viruses
   b. overdose of antibiotics
   c. lack of contact with bacteria

3. In Ken's opinion, what is needed to lead a healthy life?
   a. excessive cleaning and the use of an air purifier
   b. timely cleaning
   c. the moderate use of an air purifier

LISTENING TIPS　音変化④　同化＋連結＋脱落　 DL 28　 CD 49

自然な英語では、1文の中でも複数の音変化が起こり、聞き取りが難しくなります。

例　While I am sweeping your room, sort things out.

連結は ‿ 、同化は ⌒ 、脱落は / で示してあります

次の文を様々な音変化を意識しながら読んでみましょう。

1. Where is your vacuum cleaner? Go get it.
2. But you know what? Too clean is actually not always a good thing.
3. All we need is timely cleaning and not excessive cleaning.

III READING ACTIVITY

Adequate Hygiene

If you are too clean, is it a bad thing? Scientists have found this can be the case. They have some credible evidence to support the idea that immune-related conditions such as allergies and asthma result from excessive hygiene. People are far cleaner than ever before. This hurts their chances of being exposed to microbes, and reduces their ability to strengthen and develop their immune systems.

Over the past few decades, there has been a sharp rise in allergies. In the U.K, for instance, around one in four suffers from an allergic reaction at some point in their lifetime. This is due to the fact that modern hygiene standards have reduced our exposure to good and bad germs. Being exposed to germs helps us to strengthen our body mechanisms that keep us healthy. Being too clean deprives us of such a chance. Thus many people, especially younger people, are susceptible to immune-related problems.

Some recent research findings support this hygiene hypothesis. They show that the environment around us can affect our risk of getting diseases. Babies raised in different areas are exposed to different microbes at a very young age. The living environment makes a big difference in the types of microbes they nurture in their bodies, which in turn influences the chances of being subject to certain diseases.

Although people have to maintain good standards of hygiene, some scientific research results cast doubt on being too clean. We have to collect information to verify and determine what adequate hygiene should really be.

(253 words)

asthma「喘息」

▶ Reading Comprehension

本文の内容に合っているものにはTを、合っていないものにはFを選びましょう。

1. Scientists believe that too much cleanliness can harm our health. [T / F]
2. Modern hygiene standards help us to strengthen our immune systems. [T / F]
3. The environment around us impacts our chances of being subject to certain diseases. [T / F]

IV BUILDING VOCABULARY THROUGH PICTURES

以下の2つの単語が持つイメージをつかみましょう。

✓ influence ＝何かに影響を及ぼすイメージ

He is easily influenced by others.

Learning burnout has a negative influence on students' performances.

✓ organize ＝何かを整えるイメージ

I need to organize a trip.

He is good at organizing people.

V VOCABULARY EXERCISE

前項で学んだ基本動詞を補い、次の日本語に合わせて英語を並び替えましょう。

1. その研究によると、天候が人々の行動・振る舞いに影響が出ることが明らかになった。

[the, can, has shown, that, weather, people's behavior]

The research _____.

2. リサーチデザインが結果に影響をもたらした。

[the, design, research, results, the]

_____

3. コンサートの準備を整えないといけない。

[I, the, concert, have to]

_____

Tips on Grammar

1. I sometimes turn the air purifier on.

I sometimes turn on the air purifier. でも可能です。英語では、大切な情報を文末に置くという原則が働いており、語順によって何がより大切な情報か示されることになります。

2. Go get it.

本来は、Go and get it. または、Go to get it. となるべき表現ですが、会話体では動詞が二つ並列する形式が可能です。この場合、最初の動詞は、go, come, run が代表的な動詞であり、原形というのがポイントです。

3. Open the window, will you?

命令文に対する付加疑問文の形に慣れてください。この形式から、will you が持つニュアンスは、日本語での「〜してもらえませんか」とは異なり、押し付けが強い表現であることを理解しましょう。

UNIT 8

Does Gender Affect Cancer Susceptibility?

それぞれの性に特有な癌を除いて考えた場合、男女で癌にかかる可能性が異なります。その原因ははっきりとはしていませんが、いくつかの点が指摘されています。どのような点で違いがあるのか理解しましょう。

I VOCABULARY STUDY

DL 30 　CD 54

次にあげる英語表現の意味を表す日本語を選択肢から選び、記号で答えましょう。

1. policymaker [　]
2. Social Security [　]
3. lay off [　]
4. overindulge [　]
5. sip [　]
6. sex-specific [　]
7. morbidity [　]
8. conscious [　]
9. indifferent [　]
10. awareness [　]

a. 〜を一口飲む・少量飲む　b. 過度に〜しすぎる　c. 無関心な　d. 罹患率
e. 性別に固有な　f. やめる　g. 意識している　h. 政策立案者　i. 気づき
j. 社会保障

II LISTENING ACTIVITY　🎧 DL 31　💿 CD 55

会話文を聞きましょう。初めはテキストを見ずに聞き、次にもう一度聞いて空所に英語を書き入れましょう。

Hanako: Hi, Bob. Isn't your father's birthday today?

Bob: Yes. It's his birthday. He ¹._____ _____ _____ next year.

Hanako: You're kidding. He looks young for his age. In Japan, 60 is the retirement age. Policymakers are ²._____ _____ _____ _____ _____ _____.

Bob: In the U.S, there is no set retirement age. We can determine our ideal retirement by ourselves. Many people want to leave office around 65 and it is common for many companies' retirement plans. Currently, 66 is the age of retirement for Social Security purposes.

Hanako: It's a surprising fact. If we want to work, whether full-time or part-time, even after 60, we should be given a chance to do so.

Bob: I ³._____ _____ _____ the idea. In order for you to enjoy life and live longer, what do you give attention to?

Hanako: Eat well, sleep well, and ⁴._____ _____ _____ _____. Otherwise, we are likely to develop diseases such as cancer. Did you know that men are 60 percent more likely to get cancer than women?

Bob: Sixty percent? My father has to be more ⁵._____ _____. He better lay off the hard liquor, ⁶._____ _____ _____ _____ because he has been enjoying it a lot recently. He shouldn't have overindulged as much as he did last night.

Hanako: I thought he was just a social drinker.

(214 words)

▶ Listening Comprehension

会話文の内容について、質問に答えましょう。

1. Around what age do many American people retire?
   a. 60
   b. 65
   c. 70

2. What does Hanako suggest if we want to live longer?
   a. We need to manage stress, eat healthy and sleep well.
   b. We must not drink hard liquor.
   c. We must limit the amount of alcohol.

3. What does a "social drinker" mean?
   a. a person who drinks alcohol in moderation on social occasions
   b. a person who often goes to parties and drinks a lot
   c. a person who drinks a glass of wine

LISTENING TIPS　　h音の脱落　　　　　　　　DL 32　CD 56

機能語の中のhは発音されず、その前後の音が連結をすることがあります。この現象が起きるとリスニングがかなり難しくなります。

例　It's his birthday.　← hが落ちて、tsと次のiが連結します。

次の文を様々な音変化を意識しながら読んでみましょう。

1. He looks young for his age.
2. ...because he has been enjoying it a lot recently.
3. He shouldn't have overindulged as much as he did last night.
4. I thought he was just a moderate drinker.

III READING ACTIVITY

Gender Differences in Cancer Susceptibility

A study recently released in a medical journal in the U.K. suggests that men are 60% more susceptible to cancer than women. This study does not include statistics on sex-specific cancers such as cervical cancer and breast cancer that mainly only affect women. The gender gap in morbidity is striking and mysterious to scientists and researchers since there is no significant biological reason. They are wondering why the gender difference in prevalence rate exists.

There are two possible explanations for the difference in prevalence rates of cancer for men and women: life style factors and men's psychology. First, compared to women, a far greater proportion of men in the U.K. tend to smoke and drink. The second explanation is closely related to men's attitudes toward health. Somewhat surprisingly, men in the aforementioned study were found to be, by and large, indifferent about their health. They seem to have a tendency to hide their heads in the sand when it comes to health matters. Thus, they have less contact with health professionals.

Women, on the other hand, have more frequent contact with health professionals throughout their lives, especially regarding matters that involve contraception, pregnancy, birth, and child rearing. In addition, women's magazines are packed with a lot of articles about health and cancer awareness. If men can increase their awareness about their health and the risks of cancer, then they might be able to lower their rate of cancer.

(238 words)

▶ **Reading Comprehension**

本文の内容に合っているものにはTを、合っていないものにはFを選びましょう。

1. A recent study conducted in U.K. suggests that women are more likely to develop cancer than men. [T / F]
2. The gender gap in the rate of cancer is striking and presents a challenge to scientists. [T / F]
3. Women's magazines are filled with numerous articles about health and cancer awareness. [T / F]

Ⅳ BUILDING VOCABULARY THROUGH PICTURES

以下の2つの単語が持つイメージをつかみましょう。

 ＝目的を達成したり、成功を収めるように何かをコントロールするイメージ

We have to manage stress.　　　　　His desk was well-managed.

 ＝人の目につかないようにするイメージ

※hideの対象は、evidence, fact, tears, angerなど様々

The cat is hiding behind the curtain.　　She is hiding her inner feelings.

V VOCABULARY EXERCISE

前項で学んだ基本動詞を補い、次の日本語に合わせて英語を並び替えましょう。

1. どうしたら、こんな風になるの。帰宅して10分しか経たないのに、この酷いありさま。
   [how, you, do, it]
   _____? You've only been home ten minutes and the place is such a mess.

2. 彼は、なんとか計画を両親に知られないようにできた。
   [he, keep, secret, from, to, his parents, his plans]
   _____

3. 彼の誕生日まで彼にあげるプレゼントを隠しておきたかった。
   [to, until, wanted, his birthday, from, his presents, him]
   I _____.

Tips on Grammar

1. This study suggests that e-cigarettes help smokers to quit traditional cigarettes.

この例文のように、「研究は〜のことを示唆する・示す」という意味の場合は indicate、show、provide、report などを用い、研究の対象を明確化する場合、意味によって clarify、focus などの動詞を用います。

2. There are good reasons to support the idea.

There are ○○ reasons. の○○の位置に生じる形容詞には、良い意味づけや説得力のある意味づけができる場合は、good / compelling / strong / obvious / substantial などを用います。

UNIT 9

Why Do Many of Us Develop Fear of Heights with Age?

このユニットでは、高所恐怖症について考えます。年齢とともに高さに恐怖を抱くようになるのはなぜか考えてみましょう。

I VOCABULARY STUDY   DL 34   CD 60

次にあげる英語表現の意味を表す日本語を選択肢から選び、記号で答えましょう。

1. trestle   [   ]
2. steep   [   ]
3. acrophobia   [   ]
4. faint   [   ]
5. inhibit   [   ]
6. receptor   [   ]
7. irrational   [   ]
8. perceive   [   ]
9. reveal   [   ]
10. vertical   [   ]

a. レール   b. 垂直方向の   c. 急な、急勾配の   d. 阻害する   e. 明らかになる
f. 理解する、読み取る   g. 受容体   h. 高所恐怖症   i. 気を失う
j. 不合理な、理屈に合わない

II LISTENING ACTIVITY   🎧 DL 35   💿 CD 61

会話文を聞きましょう。初めはテキストを見ずに聞き、次にもう一度聞いて空所に英語を書き入れましょう。

On a date at an amusement park

Akiko: Wow! Look at that roller coaster. It ¹._____ _____ off the ground and along a winding trestle. It has sharp curves and steep hills. I can't wait to ride on the fastest roller coaster here.

Bob: Are you ²._____ _____ _____ it? When you ride a roller coaster, do you throw your hands in the air?

Akiko: Of course. Why?

Bob: Well, to be honest, I don't feel like riding it.

Akiko: Come on, Bob.

Bob: Well, …

Akiko: I ³._____ _____ _____ _____ this, but do you have acrophobia by any chance?

Bob: I don't ⁴._____ _____ _____ _____ what that means. Can you explain it to me in easier language?

Akiko: Are you afraid of heights?

Bob: Yes.

Akiko: Have you ever been on a roller coaster before?

Bob: Yes. When I was in primary school. I fainted after ⁵._____ _____ _____ _____ of the track. Since then, I have had fear of heights.

Akiko: Acrophobia.

Bob: Yes. Acrophobia. Roller coasters are just for thrill-seeking people.

Akiko: To the ⁶._____ _____ _____ _____, thrill-seeking people have fewer dopamine-inhibiting receptors than average in the brain.

Bob: Is that so? Well, I'd rather ride the merry-go-round over there.

Akiko: What!

(185 words)

▶ Listening Comprehension

会話文の内容について、質問に答えましょう。

1. When did Bob develop acrophobia?
   a. when he was a primary school student
   b. when he was three years old
   c. when he was a junior high school student

2. How come many thrill-seeking people are not afraid of heights?
   a. They take dopamine-increasing food every day.
   b. They understand how their diet affects dopamine levels in their brains.
   c. They have fewer dopamine-inhibiting receptors.

3. What does Bob want to ride after all?
   a. the fastest roller coaster
   b. a roller coaster for children
   c. the merry-go-round

LISTENING TIPS　音変化　同化＋連結＋脱落　　🎧 DL 36　💿 CD 62

自然に起きる様々な音変化に慣れることがリスニング力をあげるコツです。

例　I don't understand what you mean. Could you say it again?

次の文の音変化を意識して読んでみましょう。

1. Are you excited about riding the roller coaster?
2. Can you explain it to me in easy language?
3. I felt sick after we passed the first peak of the track.

Perception and Fear of Heights

Not many people jump for joy at the thought of riding a roller coaster or looking out of the window of a tall building. You are not alone. Fear of heights is one of the most common phobias.

Approximately, three to five percent of people suffer from acrophobia. Acrophobia is derived originally from two Greek words "acron" and "phobos," which mean "height" and "fear," respectively. Although such phobia was thought to be the result of an irrational fear to normal stimuli, new research suggests otherwise. Psychologists and scientists generally hold that fear of heights is an excessive response, but new studies reveal that those with an extreme fear of heights have trouble perceiving vertical dimensions.

Fear of heights often starts early in life, between the ages of 15 and 25, and it can become worse later in life. A 2016 study concerning acrophobia found that a person's fear of heights tends to grow as they age. Sixty one percent of 40 to 59 year olds and 64 percent of people over 60 were afraid of heights, compared with younger adults. In other words, older people are simply less keen on heights than younger people. The growing fear of heights is largely linked to our sense of balance and vertical dimensions. Older people tend to misjudge vertical but not horizontal distances. This misperception leads to fear and less confidence in keeping one's balance. One effective treatment for overcoming one's fear of heights is "self-help" such as staying away from the big roller coaster.

(253 words)

▶ **Reading Comprehension**

本文の内容に合っているものにはTを、合っていないものにはFを選びましょう。

1. Many people enjoy riding roller coasters. [T / F]
2. The root words of acrophobia originally came from Greek. [T / F]
3. The increasing fear of heights that older people feel is related to their sense of dimensions and balance sense. [T / F]

IV BUILDING VOCABULARY THROUGH PICTURES

以下の2つの単語が持つイメージをつかみましょう。

 reach ＝何かが伸びて届くイメージ

She reached her hand to touch his.

You can reach me by e-mail at win@abcEnglish.edu.

 **jump** ＝地面など基準とするところから上がるイメージ

※状況が「突然」である意味合いが強い

Crude oil prices jumped $15 a barrel on Monday.

The dog jumped into the pool.

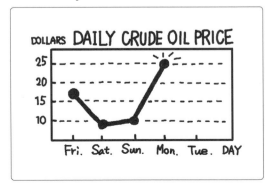

V VOCABULARY EXERCISE

前項で学んだ基本動詞を補い、次の日本語に合わせて英語を並び替えましょう。

1. お金は、営業日の3日以内に口座に届いているはずよ。
   [the, should, money, bank account, your]
   _____ within three business days.

2. 先生たちは、その計画を実行するかどうかの決断をしなければいけない。
   [must, implement, on, a, whether, to, decision]
   The teachers _____ the plan.

3. 彼は、アメリカ行きのチャンスに飛びついた。
   [chance, at, America, the, to, go to]
   He _____.

Tips on Grammar

1. It runs high off the ground.

off the groundは、「地面から離れた(ところ)」という意味で用いられています。offは、onの反対イメージを持ちます。onは「面・線に接する」が基本イメージとなります。The ship sank off Tsushima.は「船が対馬沖で沈んだ」という意味になります。

2. You are not alone.

not aloneやaloneは、よく用いられる表現です。He is not alone in suffering memory loss.(物忘れに悩んでいるのは彼だけではない)やJapan is not alone in hoping to stimulate its domestic economy.(国内の景気活性を望んでいるのは日本だけではない)のようにbe動詞の後に用いる場合や、The total number of new condos sold last year alone was 20,000 units.(昨年だけで販売されたマンションの数は、20,000戸になる)のように前の表現を修飾する形で用いられる場合などがあります。

UNIT 10
What Are the Dangers of a Sweltering Summer?

熱中症、夏バテなど暑さに関わる危険について理解を深めるとともに自分で行える対策について考えましょう。

I VOCABULARY STUDY DL 38 CD 66

次にあげる英語表現の意味を表す日本語を選択肢から選び、記号で答えましょう。

1. oppressive [ ]
2. muggy [ ]
3. humidity [ ]
4. appetite [ ]
5. fatigue [ ]
6. excessive [ ]
7. take a toll [ ]
8. prone [ ]
9. pant [ ]
10. vulnerable [ ]

a. 被害を与える　b. 過度の　c. うだるような　d. 〜になりやすい　e. 湿気
f. 食欲　g. 喘ぐ　h.（病気などに）弱い　i. 蒸し暑い　j.（心身の）疲労

II LISTENING ACTIVITY　　　DL 39　　CD 67

会話文を聞きましょう。初めはテキストを見ずに聞き、次にもう一度聞いて空所に英語を書き入れましょう。

Toshi: Hi. What's up?

Pino: Hi. Not much.

Toshi: This ^{1.}_____ _____ _____ _____.

Pino: Yeah. It is getting to me, too. Especially, ^{2.}_____ _____ _____. The weather in Nagasaki is muggy and oppressive.

Toshi: Yes. Unpleasantly hot. Steaming hot. I am very thirsty now, so let's ^{3.}_____ _____ _____ _____ _____. I really want to ^{4.}_____ _____ an ice-cold drink.

At a café

Pino: I seem to have lost my appetite.

Toshi: What's wrong?

Pino: I have no energy, and I don't feel like doing anything.

Toshi: You seem to have "natsubate," summer fatigue. Avoid drinking too much water in the summer. Too much liquid intake is as bad as too little liquid intake in summer.

Pino: I see. You're right, then; I might have summer fatigue.

Toshi: One of the major causes of summer tiredness is lack of sleep through temperature change. Have you been sleeping well?

Pino: Not really. I often wake up during the night.

Toshi: Although there is no magic cure for tiredness, in Japan we eat eel, ^{5.}_____ _____ _____ _____ vitamins A and E. These vitamins help us to overcome our tiredness and sleep better.

Pino: Most Americans are not accustomed to eating eel.

Toshi: ^{6.}_____ _____ _____ _____! (190 words)

▶ Listening Comprehension

会話文の内容について、質問に答えましょう。

1. What is influencing Pino?
   a. summer heat
   b. humidity
   c. both summer heat and humidity

2. What is Pino experiencing?
   a. heatstroke
   b. heat exhaustion
   c. summer fatigue

3. Which vitamins does Toshi suggest we take when we feel tired?
   a. vitamin A and B
   b. vitamin B and E
   c. vitamin A and E

LISTENING TIPS [g]と発音されない -ing

-ingを日本人学習者は、イングと発音することが多いのではないでしょうか。実はこの音はgではなく息を鼻から抜く鼻音の [ŋ] の発音なのです。

例 Steaming hot.

次の文をg [ŋ] の音を意識しながら読んでみましょう。

1. Let's go get something cold to drink.
2. I don't feel like doing anything.
3. I often wake up during the night.

III READING ACTIVITY

Excessive Heat Can Be Dangerous

Climate changes can be seen everywhere. The summer temperature has been rising steadily and this is no longer a laughing matter. Summer heat waves are not only extremely uncomfortable, but even deadly.

Burning temperatures through the night do not allow people to rest enough, which is responsible for the deaths of many elderly people. The elderly people are not the only ones that heat kills. It also kills young healthy people who enjoy outdoor exercise because they do not adequately recognize and understand the dangers of exercising in hot, humid weather. While enjoying outdoor sports, you may suffer from heat exhaustion or heatstroke. In these cases, you need to drink plenty of water to avoid dehydration and cool off. A high pulse rate and shallow breathing can often be symptoms of a serious condition.

Excessive heat can really take a toll not only on human health, but also on the health of pets. Pets such as dogs are also vulnerable to heat. They do not sweat to cool off as humans do, so they are more prone to overheating. Dogs try to stay cool by panting. Avoid long walks outside on a hot day. Remember that running the air conditioner in your car is not good enough for your pets. Use extreme caution with your dogs. If the weather forecast for the weekend calls for extremely hot temperatures, you need to be sure to take the necessary precautions to protect yourself, as well as your pets.

(246 words)

▶ **Reading Comprehension**

本文の内容に合っているものにはTを、合っていないものにはFを選びましょう。

1. Sweltering heat damages only the health of humans. [T / F]
2. Young people understand the risks of overheating and they are well-prepared. [T / F]
3. Healthy dogs can cool off by sweating. [T / F]

Ⅳ BUILDING VOCABULARY THROUGH PICTURES

以下の2つの単語が持つイメージをつかみましょう。

 ＝より高い位置に上がる・あるレベルが徐々に上がるイメージ

The helicopter rose slowly into the air.

The temperature climbed as the sun rose.

 ＝何かに接しないようにするイメージ

He decided to avoid the crowds.

I braked hard to avoid hitting the deer.

V VOCABULARY EXERCISE

前項で学んだ基本動詞を補い、次の日本語に合わせて英語を並び替えましょう。

1. 川の水位が上がり、町の一部が水没し始めた。
   [the, the city, and, parts of, river]
   _____ started to go underwater.

2. 彼女は、身の毛がよだつ感じがした。
   [the hairs, felt, the back, on]
   She _____ of her neck.

3. そのレポートは、物議をかもす計画に触れるのを避けた。
   [any, of, the, plan, mention, controversial]
   The report _____ .

Tips on Grammar

1. Too much liquid intake is as bad as too little liquid intake in summer.

　この文は、パラレル構造を含む文です。下線部が同じ形式となっています。オバマ前大統領のスピーチにはこのパラレル構造がよく用いられています。

　Our health care is too costly; our schools fail too many … (2009 Inaugural speech)

2. Most Americans are not accustomed to eating eel.

　この文中に用いられているaccustomed to *doing*の形式は、be動詞、become、grow、getなどの動詞に続きます。Be動詞以外の動詞を用いることで、プロセスを意識した表現にできます。His eyes grew accustomed to the light. では、徐々に目が光に慣れていったプロセスが意識されます。

3. (You) Stay cool and stay safe.

　命令文は、動詞の原形で始めると学習しますが、主語を入れて表現することもできます。All of you be quiet. なども同じ用い方です。

UNIT 11

Which Makes a Better Athlete, Being a Night Owl or an Early Bird?

朝型か夜型か、あるいは十分な睡眠を取れているかどうかでベストパフォーマンスが異なってくることを理解しましょう。

I VOCABULARY STUDY

DL 42 CD 72

次にあげる英語表現の意味を表す日本語を選択肢から選び、記号で答えましょう。

1. grip   [   ]   6. chrono-biologist   [   ]
2. early bird   [   ]   7. conduct   [   ]
3. night owl   [   ]   8. optimum level   [   ]
4. recovery process   [   ]   9. reflect   [   ]
5. biological clock   [   ]   10. sleep cycle   [   ]

| a. 最適水準 b. 体内時計 c. 夜型人間 d. 睡眠のサイクル e. 時間生物学者 |
| f. 朝型人間 g. 掴むこと h. 回復過程 i. 行う j. 反映する |

II LISTENING ACTIVITY　　　DL 43　　CD 73

会話文を聞きましょう。初めはテキストを見ずに聞き、次にもう一度聞いて空所に英語を書き入れましょう。

Amy: What's wrong with you, Mike?

Mike: I'm ¹._____ _____ _____ _____ tennis. I'm not really enjoying it the way I used to. I had tennis elbow for months and ²._____ _____ _____ _____ _____ grip strength.

Amy: Are you okay now?

Mike: I am not in pain, but my tennis level is still not ³._____ _____ _____ _____ .

Amy: Time is on your side. Don't rush to expect yourself to play better.

Mike: I know. I know. But I hate to lose.

Amy: I understand how you feel. Are you going to early morning tennis practice every day?

Mike: Yes, but I hate it.

Amy: If you are not an early bird but make a full commitment to morning exercise, it must be hard. By the way, have you been sleeping well?

Mike: I've had irregular sleeping hours lately.

Amy: Sleeping is the key to the healing and recovery process, so you will benefit from a little more sleep.

Mike: ⁴._____ _____ _____ , I just remembered that I once heard Roger Federer manages to sleep for 11 hours every night.

Amy: Does he?

Mike: Yes. Do you know how better to get to sleep?

Amy: Limiting screen time on computer or light exposure at night and ⁵._____ _____ _____ the amount of alcohol you drink will help you. Then your body will prepare gradually for sleep.

Mike: Thanks for your tips.

Amy: No problem.

(218 words)

▶ Listening Comprehension

会話文の内容について、質問に答えましょう。

1. What's the matter with Mike?
   a. his tiredness
   b. his feelings toward tennis
   c. his sickness

2. What is Mike's tennis performance like?
   a. at his previous level
   b. below his previous level
   c. above the average level

3. Which will NOT help us prepare for sleep?
   a. limiting screen time
   b. reducing light exposure at night
   c. drinking too many alcoholic beverages

LISTENING TIPS　　[t]と発音されないt　　 DL 44　 CD 74

tは、前後の環境で音が変化することがあります。例えば、アメリカ英語では、母音に挟まれると、日本語の「ら」の音に近い弾き音になります。waterが「ウォラー」に聞こえるのもこの現象です。

例　Don't rush to expect yourself to play be<u>tt</u>er.

次の文を弾き音を意識して読んでみましょう。

1. Yes, but I ha<u>t</u>e it. ←tの音が弾き音となり、その前後の音が連結するから「ヘイリッ」のように聞こえます
2. Limi<u>t</u>ing screen time on compu<u>t</u>er or ligh<u>t</u> exposure at nigh<u>t</u> and cu<u>tt</u>ing back on the amoun<u>t</u> of alcohol.

III READING ACTIVITY

Your Biological Clock

Whether you are an early bird or a night owl is not so important. Getting the right amount of sleep is more important, but it is not good enough. There is one more thing to consider: understanding your biological clock.

A chrono-biologist at the University of Birmingham in the U.K. conducted studies on what biological rhythms are. According to the results of his studies, everything we do influences the time of day that we're at our optimum level. This means our genetics, lifestyles, and patterns of behavior can be reflected in our body clock. The researcher divided athletes into two groups: morning people and night people and tested them to see whether they performed differently.

Although previous studies show that peak performance by good athletes tends to occur between 6 and 8 p.m., this was not the case in the University of Birmingham's study. The recent study indicates that morning people perform best at midday, and night people at about 8 p.m. It also shows that even morning people need a bit of time before they are physically at their best. Athletes have to understand the results of this study, and try to perform at a particular time to achieve their peak performances.

Suppose that you are one tennis match away from the championship. What do you need to do? The answer is: get up at the right time and understand when you can prevent poor performance and achieve your peak performance, depending on your sleep cycle.

(247 words)

▶ **Reading Comprehension**

本文の内容に合っているものにはTを、合っていないものにはFを選びましょう。

1. Our body clock crucially influences our performance. [T / F]
2. A recent study conducted by a chrono-biologist in the U.K. raised questions about a well-recognized assumption about peak performance. [T / F]
3. Having the right amount of sleep is more influential on our performance. [T / F]

IV BUILDING VOCABULARY THROUGH PICTURES

以下の2つの単語が持つイメージをつかみましょう。

✓ **benefit** ＝何かが誰かに対して、有利なことを与えるイメージ

We can benefit from low oil prices.

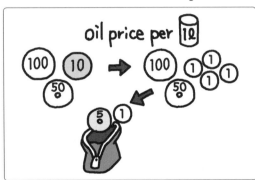

Good education will benefit us.

✓ **perform** ＝任務や仕事など複雑なことをやり遂げるイメージ

They perform the play *The Wonderful Wizard of OZ*.

The tires perform well in icy and snowy conditions.

V VOCABULARY EXERCISE

前項で学んだ基本動詞を補い、次の日本語に合わせて英語を並び替えましょう。

1. 科学と技術の進歩は、私たちに恩恵をもたらす。
[us, can, scientific, and, advances, technological]
_____

2. 若者は、栄養についての講義から得るものがある。
[young, can, from, nutrition, people, lessons]
_____

3. 私たちは、いろいろな化学物質の安全性についての研究を行った。
[a study, various, safety, of, chemical substances, on, the]
We _____.

Tips on Grammar

1. I'm not really enjoying it the way I used to.

the way I used toは、全体としては名詞句ですが、副詞的な働きをしています。類例には、I saw him that day. / She will visit us sometime next week. などがあります。

---

2. I hate to lose.

動詞hateの後には、to 不定詞の形式も -ingの形式も可能です。-ingの場合、そこには何か進行中、もしくは継続中の意味合いが存在します。I hate being back here. / I hate being fat. hateの後に -ingで表現される代表的な動詞は、be, have, go, do, getです。

---

3. You are one tennis match away from the championship.

away from ~は、あるところから離れていることを表しますが、この表現の前に時間や距離などを入れることができます。

UNIT 12
How Better to Release Your Stress?

ストレス社会といかに向き合い、コントロールするかは私たちの課題です。ストレス管理について理解を深めましょう。

I VOCABULARY STUDY

DL 46　CD 79

次にあげる英語表現の意味を表す日本語を選択肢から選び、記号で答えましょう。

1. coincidence　　　[　]
2. gallop　　　[　]
3. depression　　　[　]
4. accumulate　　　[　]
5. pathological　　　[　]
6. eat away　　　[　]
7. stress-free　　　[　]
8. achieve　　　[　]
9. ruminate　　　[　]
10. bottle up　　　[　]

a. (あれこれと) 思いめぐらす　　b. 蝕む　　c. 偶然　　d. うつ病　　e. 蓄積する
f. ストレスのかからない　　g. 抑える　　h. 達成する　　i. 病理学的に
j. 馬を走らせる

II LISTENING ACTIVITY

会話文を聞きましょう。初めはテキストを見ずに聞き、次にもう一度聞いて空所に英語を書き入れましょう。

Peter: Morning.
Mary: Morning. You 1._____ _____ .
Peter: Last weekend I was 2._____ _____ _____ _____ for a couple of hours to relax. I just wanted to be away from work. I was under stress because 3._____ _____ _____ .
Mary: No wonder you are sunburned.
Peter: How do you refresh yourself when you are under stress?
Mary: When I have free time to enjoy my hobbies, I feel happy.
Peter: What are your hobbies?
Mary: I like playing outdoor sports, especially tennis and horseback riding.
Peter: Horseback riding? 4._____ _____ _____ ! It's my hobby, too. Last time I visited Australia, I enjoyed horseback riding. I galloped a horse through a forest, across a narrow river, and over a small hill. 5._____ _____ _____ _____ _____ .
Mary: Wow! I wish I could enjoy horseback riding in wild nature.
Peter: You should try it in the future.
Mary: I will.
Peter: Stress is a silent killer, so we have to understand how better to relieve stress. When it accumulates with little or no relief, a chronic stress pattern develops, and it may create a pathological disorder, too. We need good stress relievers.
Mary: 6._____ _____ _____ _____ .
Peter: Yeah.

(186 words)

▶ Listening Comprehension

会話文の内容について、質問に答えましょう。

1. How does Peter look?
   a. He looks tired.
   b. He looks pale.
   c. He looks sunburned.

2. From what does Peter want to escape?
   a. work stress
   b. urban city
   c. a light schedule

3. When stress accumulates with little or no relief, what may happen to us?
   a. An acute stress pattern develops.
   b. A chronic stress pattern develops.
   c. A pathological disorder occurs immediately.

LISTENING TIPS　　総まとめ：英語らしい発音①

これまで見てきたListening Tipsの知識を使って、自然な英語の聞き取りができるように、読む練習をしてみましょう。

次の文を様々な音変化を意識しながら読んでみましょう。

1. I just wanted to be away from work.
2. I wish I could stay on the place for a couple of hours.
3. I got a real kick out of this movie.
4. You should try it in the future.
5. We need good stress relievers.

Silent Killer

Stress is a silent killer. It eats away our mental and physical health. It also has long-term negative impacts on our minds and bodies. Recent studies show that consistent stress can take up to 10 years off our lives, and cause potentially life-threatening disease and depression.

According to a study published in a magazine, about three-quarters of Americans are coping with intense amounts of stress, and suffering from moderate to high levels of stress on a weekly basis. Some heavily depend on anti-depressants and anti-anxiety pills to reduce their stress, but depending on such pills is not the best way forward in the long term. We have to take stress seriously and learn to reduce it in our lives.

How can we create stress-free living and achieve adequate stress relief? The answer is stress management. Coping strategies are different, depending on the situation you are in. Among such strategies for stress is keeping a stress diary. By doing so, you will recognize your stress and identify its source. Then you will avoid or reduce your stress. Another effective and appropriate way to handle stress is an emotion-focused strategy. Be positive and think positively. Deal with stressors one at a time. Never ruminate or bottle up your emotions or you may have an explosion of emotions later on. If this does not work well, communicate with people you can trust.

Managing and relieving stress is very important and useful. Stress management will help you reduce anxiety and become healthier. Don't let stress kill you!

(253 words)

▶ **Reading Comprehension**

本文の内容に合っているものにはTを、合っていないものにはFを選びましょう。

1. Stress is called the silent killer. [T / F]
2. Many Americans are suffering from stress and struggling with it. [T / F]
3. Understanding stress management will benefit us. [T / F]

Ⅳ BUILDING VOCABULARY THROUGH PICTURES

以下の2つの単語が持つイメージをつかみましょう。

 ＝悪い状況・状態から良い方向へ変えるイメージ

She needs to relieve her boredom.

The bridge relieved the traffic problem.

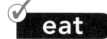 ＝飲み込む・蝕むイメージ

The vending machine ate my money.

Adult moths eat fabric.

V VOCABULARY EXERCISE

前項で学んだ基本動詞を補い、次の日本語に合わせて英語を並び替えましょう。

1. 痛みを和らげるためにこの薬を飲みなさい。
[this, to, medicine, the, take, pain]
_____

2. 彼女は、彼が自分に気づかなかったのでほっとした。
[was, that, he, recognized, had, her, not]
She _____.

3. 2, 3年のうちに、インフレが全ての経済的利益をだめにするだろう。
[inflation, will, away, gains, all, economic, the]
Within a few years, _____.

Tips on Grammar

1. No wonder you are sunburned.

この英文は、It is no wonder that you are sunburned.と同じですが、口語英語では、It is (was) の部分を省略して用いたりします。

2. I galloped a horse through a forest, across a narrow river, and over a small hill.

この英文には動詞が一つで、あとは前置詞句を用いてあります。日本語では、「森を抜け、細い川を渡り、小さな丘を超えて馬を走らせた」となり、動詞を多く用いて表現するところに英語と日本語の違いが見られます。

3. We have to understand how better [best] to relieve stress.

高校までは、how to doの形式で学習しますが、better / bestを入れる形式もよく用いられます。類似した形式にI don't know what <u>else</u> to do.やWe have to decide what <u>next</u> to do.などがあります。

UNIT 13

What Are the Differences between Real and Robotic Pets?

ロボットペットに関する事柄について学び、高齢化社会の問題について理解を深めましょう。

I VOCABULARY STUDY

DL 50　CD 86

次にあげる英語表現の意味を表す日本語を選択肢から選び、記号で答えましょう。

1. study abroad program　　[　]
2. additional　　[　]
3. leash　　[　]
4. adorable　　[　]
5. attend to　　[　]
6. aging society　　[　]
7. depopulation　　[　]
8. isolated　　[　]
9. authentic　　[　]
10. exhibit　　[　]

> a. 留学プログラム　　b. 示す、見せる　　c. 付加された、加算された
> d. 人口減少、過疎化　　e. 高齢化社会　　f. 動物を繋ぐつな　　g. 愛らしい
> h. 本物の　　i. 注意を払う　　j. 孤立した

II LISTENING ACTIVITY

会話文を聞きましょう。初めはテキストを見ずに聞き、次にもう一度聞いて空所に英語を書き入れましょう。

Andrew: Long time no see, Lisa. Where have you been?

Lisa: I **1.**_____ _____ _____ from a study abroad program in the U.K.

Andrew: Did you enjoy staying there?

Lisa: Yes, very much so. You know what, there is something **2.**_____ _____ _____ about the U.K.

Andrew: What's that?

Lisa: People can travel with pets.

Andrew: Are they in pet carriers? Do you have to **3.**_____ _____ _____ _____ for pets?

Lisa: If dogs are on a leash, they do not have to be in pet carriers, and they **4.**_____ _____ _____ _____ up to two dogs per passenger.

Andrew: Really?

Lisa: True, but there are rules for traveling on trains with pets. Animals, **5.**_____ _____ _____ _____ used to assist disabled people, are not **6.**_____ _____ _____ _____ to buffet or restaurant cars.

Andrew: Interesting. Speaking of which, I bought a dog. I named him "Win." He is really adorable. Do you have any dogs?

Lisa: Yes. While I was in the U.K., I really missed my dog, so I **7.**_____ _____ _____ _____ _____ my smartphone, which looked exactly like him. I didn't have to attend to all its needs. It just needs electricity.

Andrew: Well, I cannot tell which is better, a real or virtual pet. (197 words)

Listening Comprehension

会話文の内容について、質問に答えましょう。

1. From what country did Lisa come back?
   a. the United States
   b. the United Kingdom
   c. the Ukraine

2. When you travel with a pet in the U.K., how much do you have to pay?
   a. 10 pounds
   b. 5 pounds
   c. nothing

3. What type of dog did Lisa have while she was in the U.K.?
   a. an adorable dog
   b. a toy poodle
   c. a virtual dog

LISTENING TIPS　　総まとめ：英語らしい発音②　　

これまで学習した様々な音変化を意識し、英語らしいリズムになるように音声に続けて何度か発音練習してみましょう。

次の文を様々な音変化を意識しながら読んでみましょう。

1. I was studying at a university in the U.K. and I just came back home.
2. There is one thing that amazed me.
3. If dogs are on a leash, they don't have to be in pet carriers.
4. Dogs assisting people with disabilities can enter the store.
5. Why don't you have a virtual cat on your smartphone, if you miss your cat?

III READING ACTIVITY

Live Happily with Pets

We live in an aging society, and older adults make up a larger population than before. This accounts for the sharp increase in the segment of the older population living alone. In addition, we are facing a depopulation problem in many parts of Japan. Many older people are isolated from society and feel lonely. Robotic pets can be a potential solution to this problem.

Some older people at home and abroad have a sentimental attachment to robotic dogs. The on-board computer controls locomotion, processes sensors, and communications with its owners. Robotic dogs exhibit authentic dog-like behaviors and respond to a familiar voice, so its users can feel like they are communicating with a real dog. Owners find real comfort in this artificial companionship.

According to some scientific studies, interaction with robotic pets lowers stress, while elevating users' mood and decreasing depression. A psychologist found that brain activity increased 50% in patients who have been suffering from dementia after just twenty minutes of interaction with a dog robot. Similarly, a recently released study found that robotic dogs, used as an interactive therapeutic tool were effective in reducing feelings of loneliness among the senior residents of a care facility.

Scientists have long known that owning a pet can offer a variety of health benefits, as is shown above. Can robotic pets offer some of the same health benefits as our real dogs? When you get older and have to live alone, which would you prefer, a real or a robotic dog?

(249 words)

dementia「認知症」　therapeutic「治療用の」

▶ Reading Comprehension

本文の内容に合っているものにはTを、合っていないものにはFを選びましょう。

1. In Japan we are facing social problems such as rapid population growth today. [T / F]
2. Interaction with robotic pets raises pet owners' stress levels. [T / F]
3. Robotic pets can lower the level of loneliness of people living in care facilities. [T / F]

IV　BUILDING VOCABULARY THROUGH PICTURES

以下の2つの単語が持つイメージをつかみましょう。

 ＝地位・気持ちなど何かを上のレベルに上げるイメージ

Music elevates the spirit.

We need to elevate the position of women in society.

 ＝何かを下げるイメージ

Lower your voice.

She lowered her eyes in shame.

V VOCABULARY EXERCISE

前項で学んだ基本動詞を補い、次の日本語に合わせて英語を並び替えましょう。

1. 水の質が悪いと、下痢を伴う病気にかかるリスクが高まる。
   [diarrheal diseases, the, water, quality, risks, of]
   Poor _____.

2. 紫外線に若い頃から晒され続けると、皮膚癌になるリスクが高まる。
   [skin cancer, the risk of, ultraviolet, to, radiation, developing]
   Exposure _____.

3. 食事に脂肪分が少ないと心臓病にかかるリスクが下がる。
   [diet, risks, of, the, fat, heart disease]
   A low _____.

Tips on Grammar

1. Speaking of which, I bought a dog, a toy poodle.

Speaking of whichは、前の文で話題となっていることに関連づけて、思い当たることを述べる場合に用います。

2. This accounts for a sharp increase in the older population who are living alone.

無生物主語の後にaccount forの形式が続き、「〜は〜が原因である、〜は〜による」という意味を表します。

Review Test 2

Unit 7〜13で学習してきた内容の復習テストです。各ユニットの内容を思い出しながら、それぞれの問題に答えましょう。

Part 1

KateとToshiの会話を聞きましょう。
会話の内容に合っているものには、Tを、合っていないものにはFを選びましょう。
5〜8は質問の答えとして正しい選択肢を選びましょう。

◎ CD 93

1. Kate happened to see Toshi's father at a restaurant. [T / F]
2. Toshi's father often travels by train. [T / F]
3. Toshi's father is now traveling between Japan and the U.K. [T / F]
4. Toshi's father seems to have job stress. [T / F]

5. What is Kate's suggestion for Toshi's father?
   a. to lie on the couch and watch television
   b. to take some physical exercise
   c. to go outside and play sports

6. What does "couch potato" mean?
   a. someone who loves potatoes
   b. someone who spends most of their time watching television and videos
   c. someone who does yoga on the couch

7. What is the meaning of "die hard"?
   a. going away soon
   b. taking a long time to disappear or change
   c. leading to death

8. Which of the following is not included in the benefits of yoga described in the conversation?
   a. increased strength
   b. flexibility
   c. losing weight

Review Test 2

Part 2

英文を読み、質問に答えましょう。

Phobia: An Extreme Fear

Everyone feels anxious or uneasy from time to time. Think back to your first day of college. Your palms may have been sweating and your heart may have been pounding. These are normal response patterns to the situation. Some anxiety helps to keep you focused on something. However, when your anxiety is so serious, it interferes with you.

Air travel has become so commonplace many people think of it as routine as taking a bus was in the past, but it is not always fascinating for everyone. Many people have aerophobia, flight phobia. They have an extreme fear of traveling by plane. Studies show that at least one in five people suffers from the phobia. It can occur with anyone regardless of age.

Different factors are involved in the process of developing aerophobia in a person. A traumatic experience is one of the common causes. Some people may start having the phobia just after they see extensive coverage of a big air crash on television and Internet, or they witness a devastating crash. Other phobias such as acrophobia (fear of heights) and claustrophobia (fear of enclosed places) can trigger aerophobia.

(190 words)

英文の内容に合っているものにはTを、合っていないものにはFを選びましょう。

1. Few people regard air travel as routine as taking a bus. [T / F]
2. Anxiety never helps us focus on something. [T / F]
3. Some studies reveal that one in ten people has aerophobia. [T / F]
4. A traumatic experience can be closely related to aerophobia. [T / F]
5. Acrophobia is not associated with aerophobia. [T / F]

Part 3

英文の（　　）に入る適切な語を選択肢から選びましょう。

1. There is some (　　) evidence showing that immune-related conditions result from excessive hygiene.

2. Over a few decades there has been a sharp (　　) in allergies.

3. A study recently released suggests that men are 60% more (　　) to cancer than women.

4. A growing fear of heights is largely linked to our sense of balance and (　　) dimensions.

5. Many younger people do not (　　) recognize and understand the dangers of exercising in hot, humid weather.

6. Burning temperatures through the night do not (　　) people to rest enough.

7. Our genetics, lifestyles, and patterns of behaviors can be (　　) in our body clock.

8. How can we (　　) stress-free living and achieve adequate stress relief?

9. Managing and (　　) stress is very important and useful.

10. Robotic dogs (　　) authentic dog-like behaviors and respond to a familiar voice.

a. adequately	**b.** allow	**c.** create	**d.** credible	**e.** exhibit
f. reflected	**g.** relieving	**h.** rise	**i.** susceptible	**j.** vertical

Review Test 2

Part 4

日本語に合わせて、( )に適切な語を書き入れましょう。

1. 整理するのが不得意ね。
   You're bad at (**o**   ) things.

2. インターネットの使用状況が精神的な発達という点でどのように子供達に影響を及ぼしているか知る必要がある。
   We need to know how Internet use will (**i**   ) children in terms of psychological development.

3. 希少疾病についてのその研究から私たちは恩恵を受けた。
   The study of rare diseases (**b**   ) us.

4. よく食べ、よく寝て、ストレスとうまく向き合い、その度合いを減らしなさい。
   Eat well, sleep well, and (**m**   ) and reduce stress.

5. win@abcEnglish.eduのメールアドレスで私と連絡が取れます。
   You can (**r**   ) me by e-mail at win@abcEnglish.edu.

6. 原油価格が月曜日には1バレル15ドルにはね上がった。
   Crude oil prices (**j**   ) $15 a barrel on Monday.

7. 2, 3年のうちに、インフレが全ての経済的利益をだめにするだろう。
   Within a few years, inflation will (**e**   ) away all the economic gains.

8. その雨によって10ヶ月に渡る干ばつ状況が緩和された。
   The rain (**r**   ) a ten-month drought.

9. 私たちが行うことの重要性を上げていく必要がある。
   We have to (**e**   ) the importance of what we do.

10. 生活費を下げないといけない。
    We need to (**l**   ) the cost of living.

本書にはCD（別売）があります

Good Health, Better Life
健康的な生活から学ぶ大学総合英語

2019年1月20日　初版第1刷発行
2025年2月20日　初版第10刷発行

著者　西　原　俊　明
　　　西　原　真　弓
　　　Pino Cutrone

発行者　福　岡　正　人
発行所　株式会社　金　星　堂
（〒101-0051）東京都千代田区神田神保町 3-21
　　　Tel　(03) 3263-3828（営業部）
　　　　　　(03) 3263-3997（編集部）
　　　Fax　(03) 3263-0716
　　　http://www.kinsei-do.co.jp

編集担当　長島吉成　　　　　　　　Printed in Japan
印刷所・製本所／萩原印刷株式会社
本書の無断複製・複写は著作権法上での例外を除き禁じられています。本書を代行業者等の第三者に依頼してスキャンやデジタル化することは、たとえ個人や家庭内での利用であっても認められておりません。
落丁・乱丁本はお取り替えいたします。

ISBN978-4-7647-4078-5　C1082